Cute Little Mule

by Tina Brigham
illustrated by Paige Keiser

Decodable 17

McGraw Hill Education

Bothell, WA • Chicago, IL • Columbus, OH • New York, NY

MHEonline.com

Send all inquiries to:
McGraw-Hill Education
8787 Orion Place
Columbus, OH 43240

ISBN: 978-0-02-144935-4
MHID: 0-02-144935-X

Printed in the United States of America.

7 8 9 LCR 25 24 23

Little Mule is cute.

Cole gets on.

Go, Mule, go!

I do like to ride!

They do not go.
Mule is hot.

Mule has an excuse—no hat!

Cole has a hat.
Mule uses it.

Little Mule is not hot!

They go!